Coconut's

Joke Book

⭐ American Girl™

Published by Pleasant Company Publications
Copyright © 2007 by American Girl, LLC

Questions or comments? Call 1-800-845-0005,
visit our Web site at **americangirl.com**, or write to Customer Service,
American Girl, 8400 Fairway Place, Middleton, WI 53562-0497.

Printed in China
07 08 09 10 11 LEO 10 9 8 7 6 5 4 3 2 1

Coconut™, Licorice®, the Coconut and Licorice designs and logos, and all
American Girl marks are trademarks of American Girl, LLC.

Editorial Development: Sara Hunt

Art Direction and Design: Camela Decaire

Production: Kendra Schluter, Mindy Rappe, Jeannette Bailey, Judith Lary

Illustrations: Casey Lukatz

What's black and white and read all over?
Coconut's Joke Book!

Coconut knows that the secret to making
someone smile is to tickle her funny bone
with one of her favorite jokes!

Now you can try Coconut's jokes on your
friends. When you're through, turn to the
Joke University pages at the back and learn
how to write your own jokes that will keep your
friends giggling . . . and begging for more.

What's Coconut's favorite sandwich?
Grrr-l cheese

What does Coconut say before dinner?
"Bone appétit!"

What's Coconut's favorite summer snack?
Ice cream bones

How can you tell Coconut from a jar of peanut butter?
Coconut doesn't stick to the roof of your mouth.

What is Coconut's favorite pizza?
Pupperoni

How does Coconut eat her holiday meal?
On "bone" china

What does Coconut eat on her birthday?
Pupcakes

How do cats eat rice?
Same as everyone else—
with their mouths

What does an invisible cat drink?
Evaporated milk

What is a cat's favorite dessert at a fancy restaurant?
Chocolate mouse

What happened to the cat that drank six
bowls of water?
She set a new lap record.

What does a cat use to make coffee?
A purr-colater

What do cats like for after-school snacks?
Mice Krispy Treats

What is Licorice's favorite fish?
Catfish

Why did Coconut cross the road?
To prove she wasn't chicken!

Why did Licorice cross the road?
It was the chicken's day off.

Why did Licorice go to the beauty parlor?
She wanted to get a purr-m!

Why don't dogs make good dancers?
Because they have two left feet

Why do dogs run in circles?
Because it's hard to run in squares

Why did Coconut say "meow"?
She was learning a foreign language.

Why did the dog sleep on the chandelier?
She was a light sleeper.

Why is a dog like a baseball player?
She runs for home when she sees the
catcher coming.

How did the dog make anti-freeze?
She took her blanket.

Where does Coconut sleep when she's camping?
In a pup tent

What do you call Coconut after she sits by the fire?
A hot dog

Why was the cat so grumpy?
She was in a bad mewed.

Why are cats such good singers?
They're very mewsical.

Why do you always find your cat in the last place you look?
Because you stop looking after you find her.

Why is it called a "litter" of puppies?
Because they mess up the whole house!

What dog loves to take bubble baths?

A shampoodle!

What's white and fluffy and runs on a track?
A Cocomotive

What do you get when you cross a mobile phone and a dog treat?
A cell bone

How do you feel if you cross a cantaloupe with Lassie?
Melon-collie

What do you call a black Eskimo dog?
A dusky husky

What do you get if you cross a cocker spaniel, a poodle, and a rooster?
Cockerpoodledoo

What do you call a litter of young dogs who have come in from the snow?
Slush puppies

What do you get if you cross a sheepdog with a daisy?
A collie-flower

What do you get if you cross a dog with a football player?
A golden receiver

What goes "tick, tick, woof, woof"?
A watchdog

What do you call a cat at the beach?
Sandy Claws

What do you get if you cross a cat with a parrot?
A carrot

Why don't Dalmatians play hide-and-seek?
Because they're always spotted

Why did the Dalmatian go to the cleaners?

She was covered with spots.

What's the difference between a frog and a cat?

A cat has nine lives and a frog croaks every night!

What kind of dog sniffs out new flowers?
A bud hound

What dog smells the best?
A Scent Bernard

What do you get if you cross a hippopotamus with a cat?
A big furry creature that purrs while it sits on your lap and squishes you

What do you call a cat that swallowed a duck?
A duck-filled fatty puss

What do you call a cat that lives in an igloo?
An eskimew

What do you call a cold pup sitting on a rabbit?
A chilly dog on a bun

What did Licorice say when Coconut wasn't at home?
"Dog-gone?"

What's Licorice's favorite day of the week?
Caturday

What happened when the dog went to the flea circus?
She stole the show.

What is Coconut's favorite city?
New Yorkie

How do cats do their holiday shopping?
They place orders from cat-alogs.

What kinds of cats like to go bowling?
Alley cats

What is Licorice's favorite movie?
"The Sound of Mewsic"

What is Coconut's favorite movie?
"The Wizard of Paws"

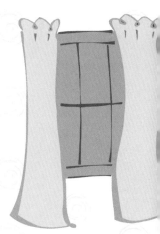

How are dogs like cell phones?

They have collar IDs.

What do you call Coconut's Web site?
A dog blog

What do you call two dogs that work in a library?
Hush puppies

What do you do if your dog eats your pen?
Use a pencil instead

Why did the dog's owner think her dog was a
great mathematician?
When she asked the dog what
20 minus 20 was, the dog said nothing.

What is smarter than a talking cat?

A spelling bee

What is Licorice's favorite class?

Mewsic

How did Coconut get to go to the ball?

Her furry godmother helped her.

What is a puppy after it is five days old?
Six days old!

What kind of dog can jump higher than a barn?
Any dog. Barns can't jump.

What kind of cat should you never play games with?
A cheetah

Who is Coconut's favorite storybook character?
Winnie the Pooch

What is Licorice's favorite color?
Purr-ple

What is Coconut's favorite color?
Grrr-een

What did Coconut say to the flea?
"Don't bug me!"

What did one of the dog's eyes say to the other eye?
"Between you and me, something smells!"

How is a dog like a penny?
They each have a head and a tail.

What does a cat do when she gets mad?
She has a hissy fit.

Where does a cat go when she hurts her tail?
The re-tail store

What happened when Coconut lost a baby tooth?
The tooth furry came.

What kind of dog always has a fever?
A hot dog

How can you stop a pup from digging in your yard?

Take away his shovel

Why do dogs bury bones in the ground?

Because they can't bury them in trees!

What kind of transportation do fleas use?
The greyhound bus

What is Licorice's favorite car?
A Catillac

What market should dogs avoid?
The flea market

Where do you put a barking dog?
In a barking lot

What's it called when one cat sues another cat?
A claw suit

Where does a cat go to pay her bills?
A fee-line

Why did the dog have to go to court?
She had too many barking tickets.

What side of a cat has the most fur?
The outside

If a cat can jump five feet, why can't it jump out a
window three feet off the floor?
The window is closed.

If ten cats are on a diving board and one jumps in the
pool, how many cats are left on the diving board?
None. They're all copycats.

Why do cats make bad storytellers?
They have only one tail.

How many kittens can you put into an empty box?
Just one. After that, it isn't empty.

What kind of cat will keep your grass cut?

A lawn meower

How do you know when it's raining cats and dogs?
When you step in a poodle!

Eleven dogs shared one umbrella, yet none got wet.
How did they do it?
It wasn't raining.

What's worse than raining cats and dogs?
Hailing hippos!

Why does the dog get so warm in the summertime?
She wears a coat and pants.

Why does Licorice wear a fur coat?
Because she'd look pretty silly in a plastic raincoat!

Why did Coconut wear red tennies?
Her white ones were dirty.

How does Coconut turn off the television?
With the paws button

What did the cat say when she lost all her money?
"I'm paw."

Why didn't the dog talk to his foot?
It's not nice to talk back to your paw.

What is the difference between a cat and a comma?
One has the paws before the claws and the other has the clause before the pause.

If lights run on electricity and cars run on gas, what do dogs run on?
Their paws

What do you get when you cross Coconut, Licorice, and an A+?

Paws-itively purr-fect pals

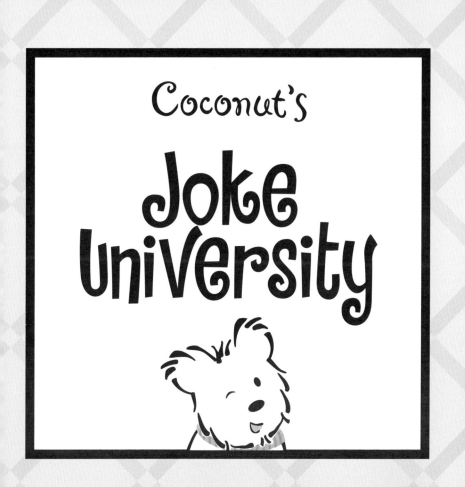

Coconut's
Joke University

The Basics

Now you give it a try. Follow these tips for creating your own funny, punny jokes.

1. Choose your subject, such as "chimpanzee." It helps to pick a word that's already a little bit funny.

2. Look at the last sound in the word, and think of another word that starts with that sound. "Chimpanzee" ends with the sound "ZEE." What's a word that starts with the same sound? "Zebra"! Mix the two together to create your punch-line word. You'll end up with something like "chimpanzebra."

3. Write a question about the two words in your punch-line word. Make sure the question doesn't actually use those two words. For example: "What's black and white, runs fast, and loves to eat bananas?"

4. Put your question and your punch line together.

What's black and white, runs fast, and loves to eat bananas?
A chimpanzebra!

You're ready to write your own jokes.

Laugh Lab

The more punch lines you think of, the more jokes you'll be able to make up and the better they'll be. Here are two more quick and easy ways to come up with your own comic concoctions:

Change one or more of the vowel sounds in the word you start with. Using "chimpanzee," you might come up with "champan-zee," "chompanzee," or "chimpunzee."

Q: What's the only jungle animal that can scare a shark?
A. A chompanzee

Replace one of the syllables in the word with a rhyming word. "Chimpanzee" becomes "shrimpanzee," "blimpanzee," or "limpanzee."

What's the
smallest animal
in the jungle?
A shrimpanzee

What's Funny?

Put some "punch" in your punch lines.

When you write punch lines, come up with as many as possible. Don't worry about whether or not they're good. Then set the punch lines aside for a while. Later on, take a close look at your list. You may realize that some of your punch lines are funnier than others. Use your funniest punch lines to write funny questions for your jokes. Tell only your best jokes. And, by the way, these jokes are best told when everyone's already a little silly!

Ha-Ha Homework

Use the rules you just learned to laugh it up using these silly subjects!

Punny Personalities: Winnie the Pooh

What is Coconut's favorite storybook character?

Winnie the Pooch

Assignment 1: Snow White

Punch Line: Snow Wait

Write your own question to finish the joke. Do the same for assignments 2 and 3. Stumped? Check the answer box on the last page for ideas.

Goofy Geography: New York

What is Coconut's favorite city?

New Yorkie

Assignment 2: Oklahoma
Punch Line: Joke-lahoma

Zany Zoology: Hippopotamus

What do you get when you cross a hippopotamus with a cat?

A big furry creature that purrs while it sits on your lap and squishes you

Assignment 3: Rhinoceros
Punch Line: Rhinoce-rust

Pup Quiz!

What's the only dog that outstinks a skunk?
A P-U-dle!

Now make up your own joke about one of these dog breeds: collie, beagle, bulldog.

....

....

....

Send us your best joke!

Write to:
Coconut's Joke Book Editor
American Girl
8400 Fairway Place
Middleton, WI 53562

Mail

Here are some other Coconut books you might like:

❏ I read it.

❏ I read it.

❏ I read it.

❏ I read it.

❏ I read it.

❏ I read it.